Steelhead River Journal

SKAGIT-SAUK

SKAGIT-SAUK

by Dec Hogan

Frank Amato

PORTLAND

Steelhead River Journal

SKAGIT-SAUK

Volume 2, Number 4, 1995

About the Author

Dec Hogan's life-long fascination with fish and wildlife has led him to a career as a full-time fly fishing guide/instructor, part-time writer/photographer. His articles and photos have appeared in several publications, including: *Salmon Trout Steelheader*, *Wild Steelhead and Atlantic Salmon*, and *Steelhead Fly Fishing Journal*. Dec began guiding fly fishers on the Skagit and Sauk Rivers in 1989. Since then he has also guided on Alaska's Alagnak River, Oregon's Grande Ronde and Deschutes rivers, and Washington's Skykomish River. Dec, with his wife Tina, and daughter Brooke, live in Mount Vernon, Washington.

Acknowledgements

For the great times we've shared on the Skagit and Sauk, I would like to thank Ed Ward, Scott O'Donnell, and Brad Adrian. I would also like to thank those who so graciously lent me a hand in the preparation of this journal: Eric Balser, Ralph Wahl, Keith Balfourd, Ian Templeton, Jerry French, Bob Huddleston, Bob McLaughlin, and my wife, Tina Hogan.

Subscription Information

One year (four issues) $35.00, Two years (eight issues) $65.00. Single copy price $15.95. (Foreign orders add $5.00 per year.) Send check or credit card information to: **Frank Amato Publications, Inc.**, P.O. Box 82112, Portland, Oregon 97282 or call 800-541-9498, Monday through Friday, 9am to 5pm, Pacific Standard Time.

Publisher:
Frank W. Amato

Editor: Graphic Production:
Nick Amato   Tony Amato

About the Cover: Spring Steelheading on the Skagit River.

All photographs taken by the author unless otherwise noted.
Frontispiece photograph: Dec Hogan
Title page photograph: Dec Hogan
Illustrations: Keith Balfourd

Steelhead River Journal is published four times per year; $15.95 per copy; $35.00 for one year; $65.00 for two years. Foreign orders please add $5.00 per year. ©Frank Amato Publications, Inc. P.O. Box 82112, Portland, Oregon 97282. For subscription information call (800) 541-9498. ISBN: 1-57188-031-3 UPC: 0-66066-00222-8 Printed in Hong Kong

SKAGIT-SAUK RIVERS

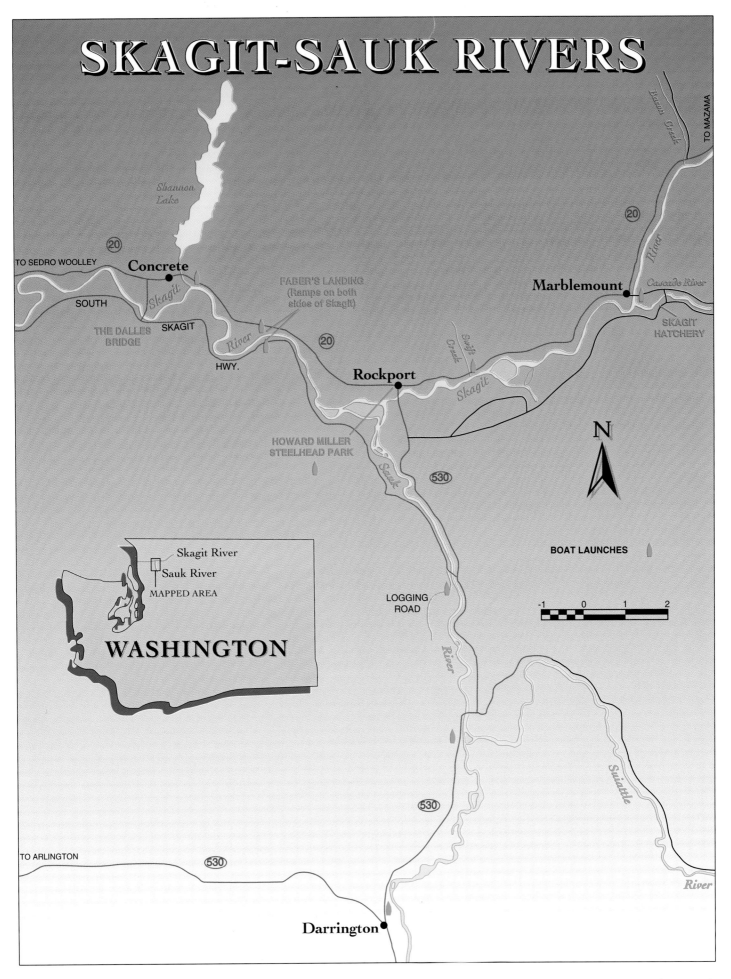

Shannon Lake

TO SEDRO WOOLLEY

TO MAZAMA

(20)

Concrete

SOUTH

THE DALLES BRIDGE

SKAGIT

HWY.

Skagit River

FABER'S LANDING
(Ramps on both sides of Skagit)

(20)

Marblemount

Cascade River

SKAGIT HATCHERY

Bacon Creek

(20)

River

Swift Creek

Rockport

Skagit

HOWARD MILLER STEELHEAD PARK

Sauk

(530)

N

BOAT LAUNCHES

Skagit River

Sauk River

MAPPED AREA

WASHINGTON

LOGGING ROAD

River

-1   0   1   2

Suiattle

(530)

TO ARLINGTON

(530)

River

Darrington

SKAGIT-SAUK

Skagit River

Of the fifteen great rivers featured in Trey Combs's book *Steelhead Flyfishing*, only two are noted for winter angling. The Skagit is one.

Few winter steelhead rivers have the necessary ingredients to be popular with fly fishers. First, Northwest rivers in winter are not the most comfortable places to cast a fly—rain, snow, sleet, hail, high water, and, sometimes extreme low water caused by sub-freezing temperatures are everyday occurrences. Second, near-freezing water means inactive fish. Steelhead are difficult enough to hook under optimum conditions let alone when rivers are running in the mid- to low thirties. So, why would the Skagit be any different? Well, it isn't, and here's where the paradox lies.

Although the fish are winter run, the season of note among fly anglers actually occurs in the spring. In fact most locals refer to these fish as spring run. Often you will hear them being called late returning winter runs. But they're not late at all; they come in when they do and that happens to be spring. True winter fishing is left for a handful of hardcore locals whose sport lies in the hooking of the occasional sea-run Dolly Varden or hatchery-reared steelhead, not to mention trying to keep the guides of their fly rods ice free.

Late in winter the first wild steelhead begin to appear. They ascend in singles or small pods, "run" being far too generous a term. As the weeks progress, fish numbers increase in a sporadic trickle. Never is there a giant push. By the time fish numbers have reached their peak in mid-April, winter, for the most part, has left the river valley and temperatures are cool yet mild. Days are longer, and a higher sun is given more time to warm surface currents, thus rendering steelhead more active. With water temperatures in the mid to upper forties, fly tackle methods become a joy.

A catch-and-release season that runs from March 16 to April 30 further adds to the pleasures. The C&R section includes the Skagit River from the Dalles Bridge in Concrete upstream to the mouth of Bacon Creek (approximately 25 river miles, not counting braided channels) and the Sauk River from its mouth upstream to Darrington (approximately 16 miles).

Lying within this 40-plus miles of river is some of the best steelhead fly water anywhere. Long shallow runs that sweep over rocky bottoms, always with deep water refuge close by, scream steelhead.

Anglers are drawn to these waters every year in search of what are perhaps the most beautiful and powerfully built steelhead in the world. It is estimated that half the run spends three or more years at sea, making for a fish that weighs from 10 to 15 pounds. Many reach the magic 20 pound mark with a few stretching beyond that. Big or small, plentiful or scarce, these are "wild" steelhead (not hatchery mutants) inhabiting the confines of this vast watershed and that is what really makes them special.

Each and every one should be regarded as an epiphany, and treated as such.

Centered in the heart of the steelhead's natural range, the Skagit is just a stone's throw from the residences of many of our sport's noted anglers. The Skagit is home water to names like Harry Lemire, Bob Stroebel, Joe Butorac, Pete Soverel, John Farrar, Mike Kinney, Dan Reiff, Ed Ward, Sean Gallagher, Jerry Wintle, and Bob Arnold. Great anglers whose names have become familiar to us through books, magazines, and word of mouth. But they are by no means the only superb anglers who call the Skagit Home.

Some of the most dedicated Skagit devotees go unheard of (maybe they want it that way) but should be recognized. They are Eric Balser, Bob Huddleston, Brad Adrian, Charlie Gearheart, Scott O'Donnell, Joe Rossano, Dake Traphagen, Stacey Lamoreux, Carl Crisp, Jerry French, Kirby Puckett, Dan Lemaich, and Wayne Cline. There are others, but these thirteen men have spent countless hours on the Skagit and Sauk during even the most marginal of conditions, thereby gaining a respect for and understanding of the rivers that can not be earned any other way. I'm sure that early Skagit pioneers Ralph Wahl, Al Knudson, and Wes Drain would be proud to know that these men carry on where they left off.

Another thing that all great steelhead rivers—summer or winter—have in common is natural beauty. The Skagit and its principal tributary, the Sauk, certainly rank highly among the most scenic rivers within the steelhead's range. Glacier clad peaks that rise as high as 10,000 feet are nearly always in view. Lesser peaks—albeit formidable mountains in their own right—plunge dramatically into the river valleys. The hillsides are adorned with evergreen trees that give way to a diverse riparian growth nearer the rivers. Myriad species of birds and wildlife inhabit the bountiful riches that such growth provides. Otter, beaver, and mink are

A large population of trumpeter swans winter in the Skagit Valley.

Sword fern springs to life

seen in and along the water's edge. While coyote, bobcat, and members of the weasel family are in abundance, they are rarely seen. Roosevelt elk and black-tailed deer bed down in the riparian tangle by day and can sometimes be spotted feeding in clearings during low-light hours. Black bears and mountain lions are plentiful but shy and wary. Although mammalian life is rarely seen among the dense thicket, a certain cast of characters brings life to the river through song and showy aerial display.

In spring the thunderous wing beats of courting ruffed grouse can be heard at frequent intervals. The haunting call of the varied thrush is forever ringing out as you search in vain to catch a glimpse of this vividly marked ground dweller. Belted kingfishers, harlequin ducks, common goldeneye, and merganser buzz the river in search of food while pileated woodpeckers pound hollow logs and cry out with a sinister laugh. Great blue heron, spotted sandpiper, greater yellowlegs, killdeer, and (if you are lucky enough to see one) green-backed herons congregate along the shorelines. Looking skyward, ospreys hunt for food, as do the red-tailed hawk, cooper's hawk, northern harrier, and raven. Spring is nesting time; the river is alive with sweet music. Walking the river trails you may be met by an angry robin as you unknowingly approached its nest too closely. It's best to keep on walking and not put undue stress on the bird.

Once on the gravel bars, keep your eyes peeled for nesting shorebirds. I often wonder how many killdeer eggs are crushed each spring by the footsteps of anglers with only one thing on their minds. Open your eyes and minds, see beyond that next steelhead. The birds of a river are every bit as magical and enriching as the fish. Naturalist John Muir had this to say about our avian friends:

"Now a wide-winged hawk heaves in sight—sailor of the air, fish of the upper sea, with pectoral fins ten times as big as his body—so high you scarce hear his fearless scream."

In all, 174 noble species of birds exist in the Skagit Basin at one time of year or another. Chief among them is the bald eagle.

During a day-long float with my friends Scott O'Donnell and Tracy Whisonant, our hopes of catching any steelhead began to dwindle fast. Rain, on the verge of snow, poured in buckets, the river was rising fast, and jet boats roared from every direction. It's a rare occurrence, but we decided to give up fishing for the day, make good time to Concrete, and duck into a warm tavern. With six agonizing miles (I know, we could have been working) left to float, we decided to count eagles, paying close attention not to count a bird more than once. By the time we reached the take-out we had counted 253 bald eagles, including one large female that nearly whitewashed us, and my boat, when she relieved herself.

The Skagit River supports the largest population of wintering bald eagles in the continental United States. As many as 600 eagles migrate from as far east as Montana and as far north as Alaska to feed on spawning chum salmon. The birds begin arriving in October, continuing to grow in numbers until peaking by mid-January. Salmon runs dictate how long the eagles will remain. In years when salmon runs are low, the number of eagles drop off by February, while a high return of salmon can sustain hungry birds well into March.

Our national symbol attracts people from all walks of life and geographical locations to the Skagit River in winter. On a typical weekend in January, eagle watchers can outnumber fishermen by ten to one, maybe more. Rafts, canoes, kayaks, and drift boats float from Marblemount to Rockport in a seemingly unending procession. Designated eagle watching sites along Highway 20 are very popular with nonboaters, sometimes getting so crowded that people are forced to park their cars along the highway instead of in the parking lots.

In an effort to allow eagles to feed undisturbed, The Nature Conservancy, which manages The Skagit River Bald Eagle Area, has implemented laws that restrict boaters from floating the Marblemount-to-Rockport stretch before noon during the winter months.

Bald eagles are a grand part of the Skagit angling experience and, no matter how common, shouldn't be taken for granted. A fishless day becomes memorable when eagles remind us of what is powerful, wild, and free.

Winter sunset near Sedro-Woolley.

Geography of the Watershed

The Skagit is one of the nation's great rivers. After the Columbia (including the Snake) and Sacramento rivers, the Skagit is the third largest river system on the west coast of the contiguous United States. The river and its many tributaries are the focus of life and energy for more than 1.7 million acres in the North Cascades—one of the most rugged and scenic mountain ranges in North America. An astonishing 387 glaciers (the most in any watershed in the lower 48 states) help feed more than 2,900 streams that tumble down from a sea of mountains into the Skagit River. The Skagit is the largest watershed in the Puget Sound Basin, and provides over 20 percent of the water flowing into the sound.

The 125-mile-long centerpiece to a 13,000-year-old ecosystem begins its journey seaward high atop the mountains of Manning Provincial Park in British Columbia. From its headwaters, the river meanders southwest through the North Cascades, dissecting mountains and landforms composed of rock ranging from Paleozoic to Teratiry in age. It then turns southeast for seven miles to the U.S. border. From there, the Skagit flows south for twenty miles in Washington. Then it heads west, breaking through the crest of the North Cascades on its way to Puget Sound.

In Washington the river basin encompasses most of Skagit County and the northeastern and eastern parts of Snohomish and Whatcom counties. To the north and to the south are two volcanoes. Standing like sentries guarding their domain, they are the highest peaks in the basin. Mount Baker (10,773 feet), which is clearly visible from almost any vantage point in the basin, is located in the northeast corner. Glacier Peak (10,541 feet), which is partially hidden from view, lies in the southern boundary of the watershed. Between these active volcanoes is a land of rugged peaks and deep valleys where summits range from 7,000 feet to 9,000. Mountains plunge to the river valley in vertical drops like 100-story skyscrapers.

Above the town of Marblemount, the Skagit watershed covers 1,380 square miles, 400 of which are in British Columbia. The upper Skagit is known for its spectacular landscapes and sharp spires. Great vertical reliefs and crested ridges give way to steep-walled valleys that are lined with cascading waterfalls. High mountain forests are home to lovely stands of Pacific silver fir and mountain hemlock. Higher yet, Alaska yellow cedar and subalpine fir sparsely decorate this harsh land.

Also located in the upper Skagit Valley is Ross Lake, the largest body of water in the watershed. Formed by Ross

Dec Hogan tails a beautiful 36-inch doe for Brian Lencho.

Dam, which was completed in 1949, the lake is 24 miles long and extends one mile into British Columbia.

Above Ross Lake the river has a moderate gradient of 14 feet per mile. Between Ross Dam and Newhalem, however, the river drops at the rapid rate of 80 feet per mile as it plunges through a gorge slicing through the rocky core of the North Cascades. Between Newhalem and Marblemount the Skagit returns to a glacial trough and again resumes the drop of 14 feet per mile.

The Skagit is fed by more glaciers than any other river in the lower 48 states.

Although angling jargon places Marblemount in the upper Skagit, geographically speaking this small town is the landmark that divides the upper and lower valleys. From Marblemount, the lower Skagit Basin covers 535 square miles as the river flows westerly through a broad valley surrounded by mountains. Between Marblemount and the river's delta in Puget Sound, the river gradient gradually eases to a rate of six feet per mile. Douglas fir, western hemlock, western red cedar, big leaf maple, red alder, and black cottonwood trees blanket the hillsides and valley floor.

The Cascade River joins the Skagit at Marblemount and is a significant tributary that originates high in the peaks of Cascade Pass. The tallest peaks in the Cascade River watershed reach to 8,900 feet.

The combined streams of the Sauk and Suiattle rivers form the Skagit's largest tributary. The Sauk joins the Skagit at the town of Rockport. The Sauk Basin covers 732 square miles, making it the largest subarea of the Skagit watershed.

As the Skagit nears Puget Sound, it slows and meanders for several miles across a huge floodplain. Eight miles from the sound, the river branches into north and south forks, then widens to form an extensive delta. At the delta, the Skagit discharges 10 million tons of eroded mountain (sediment) per year.

Whidbey and the San Juan Islands protect the delta from the force of storms that travel through the Strait of Juan de Fuca. New wetlands are created as the delta continues to grow and advance as it has for over 10,000 years. Pioneer grasses provide shelter and habitat for many species of plants and wildlife, including immense concentrations of migrating waterfowl.

Water flowing from more than 2900 creeks, streams, and rivers eventually makes its way to the Skagit.

April morning on the Skagit.

Weather, Floods, Dams and Hydro Power

The Skagit is characterized by a temperate, mid-latitude, maritime climate. Winters typically experience prolonged periods of rain; summers are dry but short. The moist marine air is responsible for moderating both winter and summer weather. The basin gets its share of nasty storms but is mostly protected by the Olympic Mountains of the Washington coast and the Coast Range of British Columbia and Vancouver Island combined.

Temperature variances in the watershed are extreme. Temperatures ranging from a high of 109°F to a low of -6°F have been recorded at Newhalem. The highest temperatures usually occur in July and August, the lowest in January. Temperatures typically drop 3°F to 5°F for every 1,000 feet in elevation gained.

The North Cascades run parallel to the coast only 30 miles from the sound. Storms moving in from the Pacific are frequently intercepted by mountains. As the warm, moist air is pushed upward against the mountains, it cools and drops its moisture in the form of rain or snow. On average, 110 inches of precipitation falls annually on the west side of the North Cascades. As much as 46 inches of snow can be deposited at elevations as low as 5,000 feet.

Precipitation increases dramatically as you move up river. The city of Mount Vernon, located near the delta, receives about 25 inches of rain per year while Marblemount, 45 miles up river, receives a high of 84 inches per year. The high mountains on the west side of the Cascades can receive in excess of 140 inches of rain and snow annually, with a record of 190 inches at Sloan

Gorge Power House helps to generate electricity for the city of Seattle.

❧ ❦ ❧

Peak. Yes, it rains an awful lot here in Skagit country.

The Skagit is a flood-prone river. Floods occur frequently and rapidly because of the vast amount of precipitation, the steepness of the mountains, and the many streams within the watershed. Skagit floods can be destructive and costly, not only at nature's expense but at our own. We silly humans have settled our homes and businesses right smack in the middle of the flood-plain!

Skagit floods come in two forms depending on the time of year. Fall and winter floods, the biggest and most devastating, occur when heavy rains pelt the valley and mountainsides. Water runs off fast and the rivers rise quickly and suddenly. Although often big and nasty, winter floods subside more quickly than spring floods.

Spring floods occur when tremendous amounts of mountain snowpack begin melting. These floods are usually smaller, but of a longer duration, than winter floods as the melting of the snow-pack can continue for a long time. Spring or winter, the worst flooding occurs when heavy warm rain falls on snow-covered mountains.

The November 1990 flood was the fourth largest since 1920 as 10 inches of rain fell on an early-season snowpack over the course of several days. Between Marblemount and its delta, the Skagit eroded huge portions of its banks, knocked down trees and swept away homes. Levees broke on Fir Island, making this piece of delta land between the north and south forks look like it was part of Puget Sound. Losses totaled in the millions.

Construction of major hydroelectric development began in 1918 when Seattle City Light was issued permits to build three dams along the Skagit River. Diablo Dam (1930), Ross Dam (1949), and Gorge Dam (1960) were raised to provide the city of Seattle with electricity. Two dams were also constructed by Puget Power on the Baker River, the Skagit's only dammed trib-utary: Baker Dam in 1925 and Upper Baker Dam in 1959. Together, the five dams can contain as much as 13 percent of the Skagit's annual discharge. The dams have helped control flood-ing, but they are usually so full in the fall that the protection they provide is minimal.

Unlike many other dams, Skagit dams have had little or no negative effect on fish passage (Baker River dams are another story and will be discussed later in this journal). The gorge where the dams are placed served as a natural barrier that obstructed the upstream migration of steelhead and salmon. Where the dams hurt fish populations is in dramatic water level fluctuations. Spawning redds are often left exposed, as are smolt and fry, when river levels are drastically raised and lowered.

❧ ❦ ❧

Huge logjams, caused by excessive logging and floods, are a common sight on the Sauk and Skagit rivers.

Fish History

When the first Euro-American fur trappers found their way to Skagit Country in the early 1800s, native people had already been enjoying a harmonious relationship with fish and wildlife of the region for more than 11,000 years. In its pristine state, the Skagit and its many tributaries were home to healthy runs of Chinook, coho, sockeye, chum and pink salmon; sea-run Dolly Varden, cutthroat trout and of course steelhead (sea-run rainbow trout). The Indians only took what they needed for their own consumption; usually it was the Chinook and coho that met these humble needs.

Today the story is not quite as pastoral. The river and its fish are presently in a state of confusion and rapid decline. If you look at the big picture it's not difficult to see why: Clear cutting of the hillsides, intense commercial and tribal net fisheries, excessive sport harvest and poaching, urbanization, high seas drift netting, dams, pollution, and all the diverse side affects associated with hatchery programs, combined or alone have all contributed, and still contribute, to the loss of fish and fish habitat.

Meanwhile, all the above mentioned species still occur in the Skagit system, although some are hanging on by a thin string. Chinook and coho stocks have been so depleted by over harvest and loss of spawning habitat that the river is now closed to sport fishing. There was a time when the Skagit was famous as a spring and fall Chinook fishery.

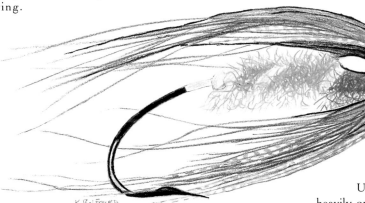

K. BALFOURD

Retired fisheries biologist Russ Orrell says that it would take 20 years of no logging to bring back suitable spawning habitat for the once prolific runs of coho salmon.

There is confusion among biologist as to how prolific the Baker River's run of sockeye salmon was. But two dams on the river obstructing passage to Baker Lake have all but made the matter trivial.

Fortunately chum and pink salmon have not been impacted by all of the abuse quite as severely and still remain in numbers close to their historic abundance. Dolly Varden and cutthroat trout are on the rebound and in fishable numbers due to enlightened management policies as well. This brings us to the river's steelhead.

Ira Yeager and Bud Meyer were the first men to guide for steelhead on the Skagit, and possibly among the first to fish for them. Good years saw in excess of 25,000 winter steelhead returning to the Skagit from late November to May. Summer steelhead filled tributary creeks, including the Sauk River, the remainder of the year—but have now dwindled to near nothing due to gross destruction of spawning habitat.

Early returning winter fish flooded the river in December and January. These relatively small streamlined fish were great biters—mortality was high. In an effort to supplement the dwindling runs, Washington's Department of Game (now Wildlife) found it in their infinite wisdom to go ahead with a hatchery program. Even though, some biologists thought the hatchery site (Barnaby Slough) would lead to a program that was "doomed to failure."

For a ten year period from the early '60s to early '70s the program flourished. Of all the winter steelhead rivers in Washington State, the Skagit was consistently ranked number one. At one time, 60 guides were licensed to work the Skagit. The catch limit was three a day and it wasn't rare for guides to run two trips a day sending home both shifts with full bags. Impact on wild fish was devastating.

Damage was done to early returning wild fish as their return coincided with that of the Barnaby Slough massacre. Anglers began fishing later and later into the season. When the hatchery run was about over, late returning wild fish bound for the Sauk River filled the need for angler's bloodthirst.

By the early '70s the biologist's prophecy had come true when a severe case of botulism broke out at the "slough." Without the aid of concrete pens (fish were reared over natural stream bottom) that could be cleaned and disinfected, it was the end of the Barnaby Slough era.

Meanwhile in 1974 the "Boldt Decision" came into effect, thereby (by court order) giving Native Americans with treaty rights the right to harvest half the annual steelhead run on Washington rivers.

Three tribes net the Skagit for salmon and steelhead: Swinomish, Upper Skagit, and Sauk-Suiattle. They rely heavily on hatchery stocks that are reared in their own hatcheries in addition to stocks from state hatcheries funded by the sale of licenses and punchcards by sport fishermen.

Following the Boldt Decision, the tribes disagreed with the state's predetermined "mimimum sustainable harvest" numbers and took matters into their own hands. The Skagit and Sauk native run of steelhead reached an all time low of 2,000 fish by the late 1970s.

Tribal net fishing was not the only culprit. Sport harvest continued at a rapid rate. That is until Washington State Department of Wildlife biologists, Chuck Phillips and Curt Kreamer, stepped in with a new management plan.

They proposed closing the Skagit and Sauk to harvesting steelhead in March and April, leaving them open to catch-and-release, no bait, barbless hook sport angling.

Phillips and Kreamer also secured agreements with the tribes to refrain commercial netting of the wild winter runs. Even though a section of the lower river was left open to kill fishing in the first half of March, the steelhead responded immediately to the new plan. The run more than quadrupled after the first spawning cycle. The Skagit was definitely on the rebound, and the future still looks bright today.

Spawning escapement recessed to about 5,000 fish by 1991, but it's thought this occurred due to drought, poor ocean conditions, or natural fluctuation. Presently, runs are on the mend once again pointing toward improved marine survival.

Early Angling

"You call it pioneering now. We called it a lot of fun."
— Ralph Wahl

Ralph Wahl of Bellingham, Washington, may have been the first man to cast a fly for Skagit River winter-run steelhead. "There may have been others, but they weren't where I was fishing," Ralph says.

Ralph was fishing for summer-run steelhead on the North Fork Stillaguamish whenever he could find time to break away from working at the family store (Wahl's Department Store) in Bellingham. Ralph had been an obsessed fisherman all of his life. When the run of Deer Creek natives would begin to stack up in clear Stillaguamish pools below the town of Oso, so would Ralph and a host of other dedicated steelhead anglers. Many of them would became life-long friends and, unbeknownst to them at the time, steelhead fishing legends.

Field and Stream magazine held a monthly "big fish" contest that ran May through December. Ralph was attentive to the fact that the rainbow trout category (steelhead were counted as rainbows) during the month of December was repeatedly dominated with entries from California's Eel River. These were large winter-run steelhead. But more important to Ralph was that they were all caught on fly tackle.

Ralph was intrigued with these fly-caught giants as he knew that the Skagit River, which was practically in his backyard, hosted runs of its own winter goliaths. "If I could figure out how to catch them, the Skagit would show those Eel boys a thing or two about big steelhead!" In 1935 Ralph Wahl set out to do what no one had ever done.

❦

Ralph Wahl was, perhaps, the first to fly fish for Skagit River winter-run steelhead. At his home in Bellingham Washington, Ralph shared with me fascinating stories of a distant era.

With persistence and unrivaled tenacity, Ralph began a blind exploration of an unknown, untapped winter fly fishery on the Skagit River. After four years of trials and tribulations on a bitter cold and often turbid river, Ralph had succeeded in his quest. One cold winter's day in 1939, Ralph beached a mint-bright buck of 17 pounds, a fish nearly twice the size of the North Fork's summer cousins. There was no stopping Ralph now, but there was still much work to be done:

"So little was known about the 'how' of this fishing, we had to start from scratch and dig it out for ourselves. It took a bit of doing to learn the moods of the big swift-flowing Skagit and to find suitable holding water within casting distance of shore (Ralph wore hip boots). It took time to get used to the below freezing temperatures and 32-degree water.

"The matter of suitable fly patterns had to be worked out. We labored over knots to use on a brand-new material called nylon. Fast sinking lines, as we know them today, were not to be had. Strong hooks were hard to come by—make do was the order of the day."

Steelhead holding in water often in excess of twenty degrees colder than that of the easily fished summer flows required the fly to be presented deep. Silk lines were dressed with everything from graphite to lead paint. Messy, yes, but worth the effort. Flies were carefully designed to sink quickly. Commercial ties were

Winter brings many rewards.

available but Ralph objected to their bulkiness for winter use. He turned his attention to the flies of California anglers Peter Schwab and Jim Pray for inspiration and designed trim-bodied hackleless flies that sank well on 2X stout hooks.

The first flies to birth at Ralph's vise were Lord and Lady Hamilton, a pair of compact optic-like flies bearing the name of a small Skagit community. The next to come was Painted Lady, a fly that was near and dear to Ralph.

"If ever a steelhead fly had grace, poise, and beauty, this is it. From the start she had a way with big buck steelhead, and weired many to their doom. Even now, a dozen years later (1957), she is still the beauty of my fly box".

Judge Ralph 0. Olson of Seattle would join Ralph on many winter forays along the Skagit River. The two men were perhaps the only winter fly fishers in the area at the time and they knew it. During the early 1940s the only competition they had along the gravel bars of Birdsview, Hamilton, Lyman, and Grandy Creek riffles, to name but a few of their haunts, was that of bald eagles. There were guides like Bud Meyers, Ira Yeager, and Cecil Jordan of Sedro-Woolley who fished their clients with conventional gear, but they would fish the deeper channels via boat leav-

ing the shallow riffles for Ralph and the judge's flies. The two would fish the Skagit almost every weekend from January through May or until the river became too high and turbid from spring run off. Entries from Ralph's journal can tell of the kind of fishing they shared.

"April 4, 1940—on a solo trip to the Skagit, I hooked 3 fine steelhead, landing a 6 and 10 pounder.

"April 11, 1940—Grandy Creek Riffle is full of fish today! In three hours I had five strikes. I beached a 9 pounder then a 9 1/2 female, the third and last fish was a magnificent one of 15 pounds that came unpinned as I was about to beach it."

Their secret didn't last forever though. By 1944 "we were marked men," as Ralph recalls. Soon other noted anglers would join in Ralph's discovery. Men with names like Al Knudson, Wes Drain, Walt Johnson, Russ Willis, and Ken and George McCloud. Of the lot, it was probably Al Knudson who first ventured forth in search of Skagit winter fish.

Each morning prior to fishing, Al would eat breakfast in a small cafe in Marysville. A few of the more inquisitive steelheaders knew this and were well aware of Al's frequent trips to the Skagit. They would conveniently be waiting for Al to show up at

Blue-pod lupine is one of the many species of wild-flowers found within the drainage.

the cafe so they might glean some information or, better yet, a begrudging-yet-welcome invitation to join him on the river. Al was reluctant to share and promptly, albeit secretly, found a new location to enjoy his breakfast.

One angler was still hot on Al's trail. Wes Drain and Al were already acquainted, having shared summer water numerous times on the Stilly. Through persistence and craftiness, Wes found himself in the fortunate position of heading to the Skagit with Al.

It was a frigid winter day in 1947, and a foot of crusty snow covered the land at the mouth of Gilligan Creek just east of Sedro-Woolley. The run had two parts. Al favored the lower gut because this is where he caught most of his fish. After finishing this lower sweet spot, he would fish the upper, less appealing riffle section before leaving. Being the gracious host, he advised Wes to take the lower section. But Wes had ideas of his own and was drawn to the upper riffle.

Al was unsuccessfully fishing his honey hole when he heard shouts from above. Wes was fast to a huge cartwheeling steelhead. After a lengthy and tenacious struggle, a mammoth buck that tipped the scales at 20 pounds, 7 onces lay in the snow at Wes's feet. The fly that soon came to be known as Drain's 20 had enticed the fish that would stand as the unofficial state record for fly caught steelhead for twenty years. It was Ralph Wahl who eventually took top honors with a fish that bested Wes's by one ounce.

At the time Wes caught his big fish, the Skagit was little recognized nationally as a trophy steelhead river. The *Field & Stream* fishing contest rules were to blame.

This was a touchy subject with the local steelhead community because the three best months to catch Skagit winter-runs were January, February, and March. The only months the contest was closed.

To thicken the plot, California's Eel River, hosted a December run of early returning fish that dominated the contest. It was thought that the rules were staged to favor the California anglers. To quote Ralph Wahl: "Open the contest January lst and the Skagit monsters will make the Eel River look like hell."

It was time to put up a fight, and so began a letter writing campaign to the offices of *Field & Stream*. But to no avail. It took a personal visit to New York by Ralph Wahl to plead for the needed change in regulations. One year later steelhead could be entered anytime of year as rainbow trout. The Skagit would finally receive its deserved recognition with numerous fish placing high in the rankings.

One such entry was a 19 pound, 10 ounce fish caught by Anacortes, Washington, resident Russ Willis. Russ, now living in Arizona, was a Skagit regular from the early 1950s on. He preferred to fish alone, but, if he were to fish with a companion, it was usually with friends Walt Johnson or Warren Erholm.

Russ and Walt had planned to spend a day in January 1959 fishing the Skagit. Rain fell heavily during the night and continued to fall as they drove to the river. At first sight of the river it was evident that it had nearly reached flood stage. This didn't discourage them however; they came to fish and that's exactly what they intended to do. Further up river, above Rockport and well upstream of the Sauk and Baker rivers, the water was still a rage, but it was running clear. Clear enough that it didn't take long for Russ to tie into his monster fish.

The only fishable water they found was in a small channel that was freshly carved by the flooding river. This is exactly where Russ found the fish. Russ and Walt knew they had an extraordinary steelhead, maybe even a record of sorts. It would have to be weighed, and quickly, before it lost precious ounces. The only problem was that it was Sunday. Any store with a certified scale would be closed.

Driving back through Rockport they noticed a man locking

A wild buck awaits release beneath the shimmer of turbulence.

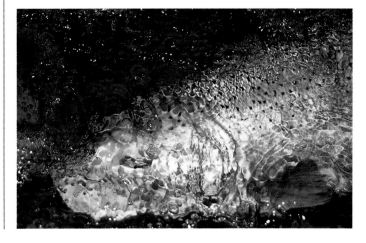

the door of a small store. Of course they quickly pulled in and explained the situation to him. Russ's luck continued to reign. The man not only had a state-certified scale, but he was also an attorney who gladly notarized the fish's weight. Russ's mounted steelhead now hangs on a wall at the Federation of Fly Fishers headquarters in West Yellowstone, Montana.

I can't honestly say that I've spent a day on the Skagit without reflecting on those great men who fished it before me. The sport is richer for their legacy. While the fishing they had was relatively virgin, crowds few and wild fish stocks not yet nearly abolished by man's greed, tackle was crude, transportation was limited, and little was known about winter steelhead. It's not hard to imagine what it could have been like with a pair of neoprene waders and a graphite Spey rod complete with modern sinking fly lines. Not to mention a four-wheel-drive Chevy Blazer and a full tank of gas.

Does it even out? They had more fish but less knowledge and inferior tackle. We have few fish, but the tools and technology that makes fishing downright easy. For me it doesn't even out. I would gladly trade in my 5 mil bootfoots and Hi-Speed Hi-D lines for a wild undisrupted fishery!

And don't think for a moment that these pioneers always had a river full of fish at their disposal. Russ Willis informed me that he once fished the Skagit (during prime time) for 25 days straight without even so much as a tug. Winter steelheading was and always will be a game of faith and dedication. With or without modern equipment.

It is impossible to go back in time. But, if you want to put yourself closer to the events of the pioneering days of the Skagit (of steelheading in general for that matter) and to better conjure up a mental image of the past, I strongly suggest you view the photography of Ralph Wahl.

Ralph never went fishing without a camera, and his black-and-white photography catches the essence of steelheading like no other. At a time when people just like you and me were running around steelhead rivers, fly rod in hand, trying to catch a fish, Ralph had the foresight to realize just how important an era of steelhead fly fishing was unfolding. "I don't think the others knew what was going on—they were just happy to be fishing. I knew it was something special."

Ralph's wonderful book, *One Man's Steelhead Shangri La* (Frank Amato Publications, Inc.), recounts Ralph's early fishing days on the Skagit River and tells the tales of a backwater slough that would be Ralph's secret steelhead Mecca for more than 40 years. His striking photos grace the pages of that book and two other books of note: *Steelhead Fly fishing and Flies* by Trey Combs (Frank Amato Publications, Inc.), and *Come Wade the River* (no longer in print), a beautiful book of Ralph's photography complemented by excerpts from the writings of Roderick Haig-Brown.

K. BALFOUR

Fishing

The Skagit is classic big water with a lot of places for steelhead to hide—many of them not within reach of a fly. In fact, most of the holding lies are better suited to other methods of angling. When viewing the river from a nearby hillside, I still find it hard to believe that we ever take fish on flies in the Skagit.

Fortunately, many of the steelhead that travel up the Skagit do so close to shore and out of the main flow of the current. This "path of least resistance" is what to look for when seeking suitable fly water. In effect, we are fishing for traveling steelhead. The best places to fish are those that force the steelhead to slow down or stop: a fast shallow riffle that slows and deepens, the tailout above a long fast stretch or heavy rapid, the first deep slot above an expanse of shallow nondescript water, etc.

If the river bottom is made up of good-sized rocks and boulders, it usually makes for a more attractive holding lie, but big rock is not entirely necessary to hold a traveling steelhead. As long as the bottom is hard (not sand or silt) with cover in the form of depth or a choppy surface, it's worth a look. Remember that the operative word is "traveling". Therefore, a pool or piece of water that is void of fish one hour may hold one or more the next.

I remember driving down a narrow path to fish a favorite run and meeting another angler's vehicle as he was leaving. He seemed discouraged. "I wouldn't even waste my time Dec; I just fished through twice with nothing," he moaned. "Besides, when I got there Farrar was guiding a couple of clients, and they didn't touch a thing either," he said.

I just smiled and gave him the customary, "I'm just happy to be out" line, which was very true. And that's probably why—in a run that I now had all to myself—I hooked two steelhead.

Where water depth is concerned, two feet is not too shallow and eight feet is not too deep, three to six being about perfect. Where many people cheat themselves of a possible fish (maybe the only one in a day's efforts) is in the two to four foot range. Skagit fish will hold in surprisingly shallow water, particularly in low light or in a well rested piece of water. Remember, if the water is two-feet deep with enough flow to swing a fly, it has potential.

The fish that takes your fly in two feet of water may not have actually been holding there. He may have followed and decided to take the fly when it came to a stop. By not wading too deep, you may have allowed the fish more time to make his decision to take the fly. Fish your cast thoroughly.

In addition to cheating yourself by excessive wading, you can certainly cheat other anglers. Sloppy wading may spook fish, pushing them into greater depths. It might also inhibit newly arriving fish from taking up resting stations close to shore. If you want to make enemies in a hurry on the Skagit—wade a little

deeper. If you haven't fished big water before, it might be intimidating. You may feel the fish are always out of reach. And, who knows, maybe they are. But, rather than mucking things up for those who may be fishing behind you, it makes more sense to sharpen your casting skills. Even the Skagit anglers who are not known to throw a long line still cast 50 to 55 feet on average. I did a quick study one day and found that out of the six runs I fished (four on the Skagit, two on the Sauk) the average successful distance I covered was 75 feet.

Skagit River wild steelhead are very aggressive by nature, being referred to by the locals as "biters". When they take the fly it is often very strongly, sometimes even violently. Your fly is swimming along nicely when all of a sudden the line snaps tight and the reel starts screaming before your brain has time to process what's happened. While the fish will sometimes follow the fly great distances before taking it, more often than not the fish rises to meet the fly with a crushing blow shortly after it starts to swing. I have experienced some very startling grabs over the years—vigorously stripping in line to make a new cast when WHAMMO loose coils are ripped from my line hand like a retractable power cord. Sometimes the take is so sudden it's as if the fish saw the fly in flight and jockeyed into position to make an athletic interception when it hit the water. This take always leaves me gasping for air.

Because these steelhead move readily to take a fly, it is apparent that "hitting 'em on the nose" is not necessary. The right line is important. If the line and fly are extremely heavy, it becomes difficult to fish a broad thorough swing.

Floating by driftboat or raft is a popular way to explore the Skagit and Sauk.

The soft inside seam where steelhead like to hold is often too slow and shallow to keep a long heavy shooting head fishing. With such a line the angler spends more time breaking off snagged flies than fishing them.

Skagit River near Concrete.

Guide John Farrar, instructing one of his many students on proper presentation.

Sink-tips in the ten- to fifteen-foot range and unweighted flies are the bread and butter of Skagit fishing. A 13-foot Scientific Anglers (type 4) sinktip, or it's equivalent, in an eight or nine weight, is all one needs to cover the water effectively. The length and density of these tips combined with the buoyant floating belly section allows the angler to control the line at a multitude of speeds, angles and depths. Most experienced Skagit anglers will carry several tips in a variety of lengths and densities, but it would be safe to say that everyone has a pet line that does the bulk of the work.

Winter or spring, the Skagit is best fished by starting at the top of a run and finishing at the extreme tail, covering everything in between through a series of step-casts. Once the run has been fished, it is often wise to move on in search of new water. There are, however, times when a second pass may not be a bad idea. The first, and most obvious, would be if you hooked a fish on the first pass. Here it is certainly wise to change flies and fish through again. It is also hard to leave if fish are seen rolling, particularly in the tailout. Frequently, fish you see entering a pool at the tailout can be hooked once they slow down at the extreme head of the run, or in the buckets.

During the cold of winter, steelhead can be very lethargic. Often it may be necessary to fish a run several times at a slow pace to satisfactorily cover the water. The days are short and it isn't rare to devote the better part of a day to fishing one piece of water. On the other hand, you could take the "cover as much water in a single day" approach in search of the anomalous active cold-water biter. The choice is yours. I have used both approaches with equal successes and failures.

I am often asked, "What's the best way to catch steelhead on the Skagit and Sauk?" The people who ask this are obviously searching for some technical answer that will make a difficult quest much easier. In truth, the answer lies in our willingness to open our whole mind, body, and soul to becoming part of the river. Once you become one with the river, there is no holding back. Should mental dams arise—tear them down and keep going.

Steelhead fishing is all about discipline. Relish the anticipation. Visualize your fly as a living entity while you move in a Zen-like trance. See yourself hooking a fish on every cast. If you are doing it right, you will be relieved of all negative anxieties. You won't wonder if the fly you are casting is the right one. You will be perfectly content with the line you selected. More importantly, you can't help but enjoy yourself. I see a lot people who are so uptight about hooking a fish that they forget the real reason they are on the river. If, in fact, the reason IS just to hook a fish, maybe it's time to take up a new form of recreation. Steelhead to a fly is a high art form, and a privilege that is not always attainable at our beckand call.

Flies for Skagit Country

It would be easy to fill a fly box with patterns that would see you through a winter season in Skagit country. In fact, it wouldn't have to be much different from a box bound for any other winter river, or summer river for that matter.

A box of summer-run wet flies for, say, the Deschutes River in Oregon would consist of some dark flies such as Skunks or Night Dancers, a few bright flies such as Skykomish Sunrises and Fall Favorites, and, of course, some neutral patterns such as Burlap or Lady Caroline.

With the flies tied in larger sizes, 2 to 2/0, this Deschutes summer-run box would be perfectly suited to tackle the Skagit and its varied conditions throughout winter.

Unlike many other great steelhead rivers the Skagit does not have a fly or list of fly patterns that is instantly synonymous with its name: Such as the Thompson River and the Doc Spratly; the North Umpqua and the Green Butt Skunk, Black Gordon and Umpqua Special; the Deschutes with its Freight Train and Mack's Canyon; the Skykomish and the Skykomish Sunrise.

A look inside the author's fly box. Steelhead are not picky, tie as the spirit moves you.

Red and Orange Marabou
(Dec Hogan)

Purple Marabou
(Dec Hogan)

Black Marabou
(Dec Hogan)

Red Eagle
(Joe Rossano)

Proweler
(Dec Hogan)

Bat-Ray (top view)
(Scott O'Donnell)

Seizure
(Eric Balser)

Intruder
(Ed Ward)

General Practitioner
(Mike Kinney)

Goose Creek
(Charlie Gearheart)

Usk Grub
(Dec Hogan)

Green-Butt Skunk
(Harry Lemire)

Coast Orange
(Dec Hogan)

The flies of the Skagit's pioneering fly fishermen like Ralph Wahl, Al Knudson, and Wes Drain are as close as we can come to establishing fly patterns synonymous with the Skagit. Unfortunately, the patterns of these great men are not in use on the Skagit today, nor can they be found in the local fly shops. If a person is found fishing a Painted Lady, a Knudson's White Marabou, or a Drain's 20, it is usually out of respect, honor, or a desire to connect with the past.

The Skagit's core of anglers is and always has been made up of unique individuals who tend to be leaders rather than followers. With so many leaders it's no wonder that most of the flies that break the Skagit's surface are unique to the person who casts them. The fish don't seem to care what we throw at them, so why shouldn't we experiment and innovate to make our flies truly ours?

Flies are half the fun of the sport. It's a fascinating thing, a steelhead fly. Unlike trout fishing, where the game of match the hatch is so often crucial to ones success, steelhead fishing has no "right" pattern. Actually, the right pattern is the one you're using. And, for whatever reason you choose to fish that fly, the reason is right.

We are free to design and tie flies to satisfy our whims and convictions. Harry Lemire's flies are not very big or intrusive as they blend in and complement the river color. Ed Ward's flies look like behemoth sea monsters right from the pages of a Jules Verne novel. Both men have justifiable reasons for fishing their flies and both men catch fish. So, we tie to satisfy our own convictions. If it's tradition you want, go ahead. If you like a certain color and want to see how its hue coordinates with that of a steelhead's jaw, all the better. Or, if you're like me, you want to catch as many fish on as many different patterns as possible (keeping within certain parameters suggested by my own convictions of course). If our flies match our convictions, we will fish them with confidence.

Although the Skagit crowd is made up of individuals who fish their own patterns, that's not to say that our styles and ideas don't rub off on each other.

Prawns, Speys and Marabous

Much has been written about the eyesight and behavioral characteristics of steelhead. The majority of that information has been gathered not by scientists but by inquisitive anglers just like you and me. When we process this data and incorporate it into our flies, it's not so much science as it is romantic speculation. I know of one angler who believes that the color of his hook is critical to his success. Although it's probably far from the truth, I can't help but respect his opinion. The mysteries of steelhead drive us to formulate many opinions, both founded and unfounded. These opinions keep us going as we pursue the secrets of steelhead. With this in mind, let's talk about the flies Skagit River steelhead are caught on.

Presently, the majority of flies being used in Skagit country come in three basic styles: prawns, marabous and Speys. And, yes, all variations, combinations, and marriages of the three. Flies ranging from a simple clump of marabou lashed on a hook to elaborate works of art all take fish regularly. It is the shape and action of the dressing that really counts. And this is why prawns, Speys and marabous take top billing.

If you look at the Skagit as an extension of the ocean, it's easy to see why these styles are so effective. They all have a prawn, or squid-like shape and movement. They mimic the very food steelhead are conditioned to eat. When steelhead enter the river, the conditioned reflex to react quickly when food presents itself remains strong. And, if that's too much "romantic speculation" for you, let me put it this way. They work!

Another reason for the popularity of Speys and prawns. Aside from their appeal to fish is that they often appeal aesthetically to the angler. I don't know of any Skagit angler who doesn't appreciate the grace and elegance of a well-tied fly. Embellishments and all.

Almost everybody fishes a fairly large fly with a lot of built-in action such as Bob Aid and John Farrar's marabous, Spey flies of varying degrees of fullness, and endless variations of the General Practitioner. Black, orange, and purple get top billing as the most popular colors. And Alec Jackson's Spey hooks wear them well.

I like to think of Skagit country as the land of freestyle fly tying where people cut loose from their inhibitions at the tying bench and just let it roll—whatever happens, happens. With a massive ocean like the Pacific, an immense river system like the Skagit, and a mysterious sea-going fish that returns to rivers not for food but for spawn, one can't help but let the imagination run wild when tying flies.

Spey Rods

Each generation of angler has left a significant mark on the sport of steelhead fly fishing. The earliest generation was the first to pursue and take steelhead on the fly. Later groups began developing fly patterns that are still in use today—some are classics that will remain forever. A newer generation made, perhaps the most important breakthrough in the developments that led to the taking of winter-run steelhead on fly tackle—sinking lines and shooting heads.

These are just a few examples of the fingerprints left by previous generations. There are many more and, provided remaining stocks of wild steelhead are cared for properly, future generations will continue to leave their mark through innovation and exploration.

When I look to see what my generation (the NOW generation) has contributed and will pass on, several things come to mind. But the popularization of the Spey rod is perhaps the most significant.

Certainly the now generation can't be given credit for inventing Spey rods; two-handed rods have been in use for several cen-

Two-handed rods are popular with Skagit anglers.

turies throughout Europe, including Scotland where flows the River Spey itself. Nor can we claim to have been the first to cast Spey rods on steelhead rivers; Roderick Haig-Brown writes of

Fifteen-year-old Mark Fitterer learning to Spey cast, as day breaks on a foggy April morning.

27

Every season a few steelhead topping 20 pounds are hooked by fly anglers. It should NOT, however, be expected.

fishing for steelhead with two handed-rods in his 1939 book, *The Western Angler*. But the mid-1980s to the mid-1990s should be remembered as the revolutionary era of Spey fishing for steelhead.

No single individual should be given credit for introducing the Spey rod to steelhead rivers. More than likely several people discovered the virtues of the Spey rod independently and began experimenting on their respective home waters. Fortunately, some of these individuals are well-known and respected anglers with names like Jim Green, Mike Maxwell, Jim Vincent, Harry Lemire, Pete Soverel, John Hazel and Mike Kinney. These anglers and the rods they use didn't go unnoticed. At present, most of the major rod manufacturers offer several two-handed rods that use modern technology and graphites in their design and construction.

The Skagit River has been a testing ground and ignitor of the Spey rod explosion over the last decade. With its big, wide runs that sometimes require a long cast to be covered properly, its many high-bank holding lies where trees come right down to the river's edge, and, of course, its who's who of dedicated winter steelheaders, it's only natural that the Skagit would be at the center of modern Spey fishing.

Five years ago I could have easily listed the names of those who regularly fished the two-hander on the Skagit and its surrounding rivers. Today, however, it would be far less laborious to list those who don't, for they are few in number. It's true that people did just fine fishing the Skagit without the aid of a Spey rod. But you can bet that those who are avid proponents of its merits would probably rather stay home and watch reruns of "Gilligan's Island" than to fish the Skagit without their two-hander.

The Big One

Even a small steelhead is a big fish when caught on fly tackle. If steelhead never grew beyond eight pounds, it is doubtful they would be any less important as a gamefish. Wide-eyed hopefuls would still spend lots of dollars on tackle and equipment and would still travel, sometimes great distances, to use it. The writers would still write, the tiers would still tie, and fly reels would still need to hold at least 150 yards of backing.

A healthy population of native sea-run Dolley Varden exists within the watershed. Dollies are a regular incidental catch when steelheading. Each one is a welcome prize, and should be released unharmed.

The hazy glow of a winter sunrise near Hamilton.

⌘

But steelhead do grow to be more than eight pounds. In the back of our minds lurks the exciting possibility that our next fish might be The Big One.

I don't want to fool you into thinking that hooking one is an everyday occurrence, because it isn't, but the Skagit is a river of big, sometimes enormous, fish. Most of those who have fished the Skagit and Sauk for any length of time can share tales of fish that went 20 pounds or better. Some landed, most not.

Not all of the fish said to break the magic 20 pound mark are for real, however. Steelhead stir emotions and just the sound of the word "steelhead" elicits some form of emotional response from those who are even vaguely familiar with fish. Say "bird" to a good Labrador retriever and you'll see what I mean. At the very least, he'll perk up his ears and snap to wide-eyed attention. But, more often than not, he'll shake and wiggle like a child standing in front of a well-stocked candy machine. He may even pick up the nearest object and parade around drooling proudly over his mock prize. This has also been known to happen to the occasional good "steelhead retriever." And with no wrongful intent, this is where the truth, like a flyline tangled in a rootwad, gets stretched.

If the largest steelhead a person has ever caught is 10 pounds and suddenly they are connected to an honest Skagit River 15 pounder, they might think they have a whale. And they do. A 15-pound steelhead is a big animal—but its not 20. And so the story goes, whether it was landed or not: "This fish was HUGE -had to be at least 20." A fish that powered off with enough back-

ing to encircle an 18 wheeler but came unhooked before it was seen is a prime candidate for: "Did you see that!" (Heavy breathing.) "That thing had to be HUUUGE!" Sure enough, after several hours of contemplation, another 20-pounder story hits the network.

But some of the stories, like the anglers who tell them, are for real. Such is the case with Jerry Wintle and his legendary steelhead.

Jerry is a Canadian from British Columbia who is respected as one of the best steelheaders alive today. Every April, Jerry, accompanied by his wife, Jean, pulls his Airstream trailer down from B.C. to fish the Skagit's catch-and-release season. To those who know Jerry and Jean, their arrival at Howard Miller Steelhead Park is cause for celebration. Just like the sound of grouse drumming in lust, the scent of cottonwood trees giving birth to sparkling new leaves, and the sight of violet-green swallows catching mayflies, Jerry and Jean Wintle are another sure sign that spring has begun on the Skagit.

On the last day of the 1989 season, history was made when Jerry hooked and landed a monster steelhead that measured an incredible 48 inches. Why was history made? Because he knocked a couple inches off the true measurement to arrive at 48—surely nobody would believe a 50-inch steelhead. Forty-eight is hard enough to believe, but it happened to Jerry Wintle, and he's as reliable as they come.

When news began to spread of this steelhead of steelhead, I doubt there was anyone who didn't secretly wish they had caught it themselves. My initial reaction was one of disbelief, which

⌘

Howard Miller Steelhead Park in Rockport accommodates tent campers as well as trailers and R.V.s.

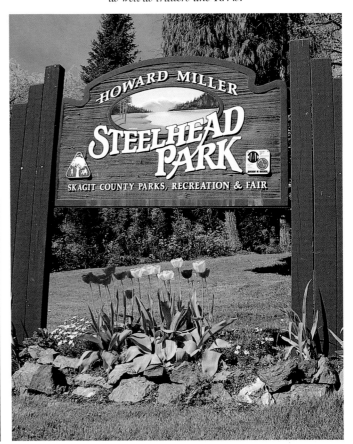

29

Typical riverside forest.

You never know when luck will come your way. Like snow on your hat, it piles up quietly and you never even know it's there. Then, when you turn your head just so, it all falls down your neck. That's the way it seems to work. Luck, nature, odds, whatever you may call it, that's how it happens—if it happens at all. Here are a few first-hand stories from some of the Skagit's Lucky ones.

Spirit to Share
Jerry French

The day was perfect—gray skies, the river a deep green. The smell of budding cottonwoods helped to inflate my spirit. It didn't hurt that I had taken the months of March and April off from work; I was fishing every day.

With no worries, Scott Howell, Ed Ward and I looked over the water we were about to fish. We would share two long runs. Scott and Ed would split the uppermost pool; the bottom run was all mine.

The run before me comprised a fast head, broken up by large rocks, that spilled into a very spooky gut section that was followed by a classic tailout. As I was planning how I would fish the run, I noticed a large softspot formed by a submerged bar. It looked like a steelie hotel. I decided to wade out and fish it first.

The wade was not fun. Later, Scott said that I looked like I was "break dancing" as I moved through fast, waist-deep slots containing big rocks.

Standing 40 yards from shore with fast water swirling all around me, I started to fish. I never once considered what I would do should I hook one.

The lie was about 30-feet wide, 60- to 70- feet long, and full of rocks. I made a short cast and it fished great. I figured that after I had worked into a good long cast I could make six or seven step-casts before the hole was too deep to continue. As the fly swung below me on the first long cast, I felt a dull pull. The pull continued to build pressure, so I set hard.

For a second I thought I was snagged. Suddenly my snag rushed into the fast current and turned down river. I tried to stop the fish, turn it, and get it back into the soft spot. No luck. My backing began to leave the reel even faster. Thoughts of the predicament I was in filled my head as I moved down and found myself up to my armpits in water. I was slipping downstream with my waders filling; the fish ran on. I carefully backed up to the soft spot and crossed back to shore the way I had waded out.

quickly changed as that tinge of petty jealousy wormed through my veins like a river on the rise. I'm sure that my reaction was the one shared by all. Ultimately, if it couldn't be us, everyone agreed it couldn't have happened to a more deserving man than Jerry Wintle.

Had such a fish been killed and weighed (it was, of course, released), more than likely it would have shattered any and all existing records for steelhead. We can hope this great fish went on to spawn and spread his special genes.

There are numerous accounts of big fish being caught on the Skagit and Sauk rivers. And though the possibility exists that you might catch one, it should never be expected. This is where luck comes into play.

Steelhead spawning in small tributary creek.

❦

The second crossing was twice as bad as the first. I was fighting a fish I had not seen and did not believe was hooked well. We all know that a fish hooked on the "hangdown" usually results in a lost steelhead.

I walked downriver, frantically trying to collect some backing, and myself. Soon I got some running-line back on the reel. That's when I could see a huge chrome shape the size of a car bumper. I tipped the fish back and forth hoping to wear it out. It seemed to be working until the fish ran off with another great deal of backing.

It had been a long fight and I feared for the fish's survival. At the risk of losing this mysterious fish, I pulled back near to the breaking point of my ten-pound tippet. Soon the fish lay on it's side in the shallows.

I can't describe how I felt when I saw how massive the fish was. Massive is a good description—39-inches long and the girth of a Thanksgiving ham. The most massive hen that I had ever seen or heard of.

I took a couple of pictures and set her free. She swam away as if nothing had happened. I stood there all wet and sweating with trembling arms and a smile the size of Texas.

Thoughts of her, the battle, and the wonderful gift she was took me over. So I sat for a moment right there on the rocks with my feet in my beloved river. I said out loud, "Thanks." Not for the big fish, but for the life I lead as a steelheader, for living in Steelhead Country, and for the opportunity to share a moment in that fish's life.

I feel that I gain some of the spirit of every fish I hold. I will always remember her for the experience and piece of spirit she gave me. Oh, yes, and for her size.

The Gift
Bob Huddleston

We come to the river seeking gifts, and, if we seek with all our senses, all our spirit, these gifts are many. The bark of a coyote, the shadow of an osprey, the soft buds of spring willows. Many people demand and will accept only gifts that they deem significant. To demand the fight of a fish and to accept no other is to fish in darkness.

❦

Skagit steelhead will test the limits of your tackle, every time.

Columbia lilies and Web.

* * *

There are places along all rivers where the woods stop and the river begins, a last place of dark sanctuary before stepping out on the naked bar. A place where the sweat cools after a hard walk, a place to find quick shelter from blasting wind, driving rain and scorching sun.

I always pause for a moment at this place. I pause as if standing before some unseen doorway, looking out upon the bar, watching and waiting as if the quiet mystery of the river will suddenly unfold. Lingering in these shadows, looking out over the gray stones and bleached drift to the flowing river, I find hope.

Sometimes the bar has other anglers on it, and I watch how they fish before they know I am there. Sometimes I turn and leave; sometimes I join them.

The river had been out for weeks, swollen and brown with late-March rain. The first week of April had come sunny and warm. Along the bar a thin strip of clear green water flowed next to the brown main current. Below the bar the two flows mixed into a broad brown sameness that sickened the hearts of less knowledgeable anglers. This knowledge was given to me by another angler. "Go to the place at first light," he had said, "and the water along the bar will flow clean."

Wading slowly into the shallow riffled top of the drift, I began with short casts. A dozen short casts into the drift I felt a light pull. Taking a step backwards I cast again and the river answered with the throbbing weight of a fish. A good fish. Not a particularly big fish nor a particularly strong fish, but a good fish nonetheless. It fought admirably as the sun peeled the morning clouds away from Sauk Mountain. Bringing it into the shallows, I noticed the stubbed dorsal. A hatchery fish here in the sanctified catch-and-release wild fishery. It was a nice bright spunky hen of about nine pounds. An anomaly the biologist said couldn't exist, or, in their guarded terms, "The overlap between hatchery and wild fish is expected to be minimal." It was fun catching the fish but now things were becoming complicated. The joy of catching the steelhead became diminished by an ethical and moral dilemma. This fish should be killed, yet the regulations forbade it. I was alone and could easily kill the fish and thrown it back in the river, yet my conscience would not let me. I could sneak it back to camp and eat it, but then I would be considered a poacher. Loosening my grip around the wrist of its tail, I watched the fish swim easily back to the sanctuary of the wild.

A good fish is always a blessing and I began casting again, lengthening my strokes, leaning into the casts, shooting for distance as I moved into the bucket. I had taken a fish and even though the thrill was diminished somewhat by the steelhead's origins, I had still taken a fish. I now became aware of the other gifts the river had to offer—the coldness of the air against the river's surface, the cloudless day, the turn of the hillsides into the green of spring.

I had attained the cast step rhythm of steelhead fishing with the fly. I needed nothing but the feel of the rod, the pressure of the river against my legs, and the sweet enjoyment of the drifting line. Then something slammed the fly hard. Pulling back on the rod I felt the deep throb of strength that said I was no longer in control, the flush of warm breath that told me I was nothing amid the flow of the river and soar of the heavens.

This was more than a good fish. It was the kind of fish that forever imprints the coldness of the river, the feel of the sun, the green of the trees, and the gray of the stones on the synapses of

* * *

Fishing is prohibited downstream of the Dalles Bridge during the Catch-and-Release season.

Skagit angler Scott O'Donnell holds a wild doe that is the epitome of Skagit country steelhead.

memory. A fish that etches the moment on the fabric of your spirit. It is from this that the legends flow, not from length, girth, or weight but the perceptible welding of moment to memory. I will forever feel the hard stones on weak knees as I knelt in the shallows cradling that steelhead in my hands. The broad high sweep of its dorsal was a connection to the wild, to broad sweeps of dark ocean. On that day everything became different. On that day everything became new again.

Big Weird Salmon
Eric Balser

Sometimes the events leading up to a special day are anything but special. Sometimes they can be negative or flat-out bad. That's how things started for me when I went up the river one March day eight years ago.

As usual, the rain and warm temperatures started two or three days before my day off from work, leaving me with little hope of finding fishable water. But, being a fisherman, all I needed was that little bit of hope.

At dawn I was standing at the head of the Picnic Table Run on the Stillaguamish River watching brown foamy water rage through the willows. The same willows you stand in front of to fish at normal flow. I was angry at myself for knowing better, but not doing better.

At this point I was too disgusted with myself to go home. Instead, I decided I should try, no matter what, to find a place to fish. I remembered what Mike Kinney had told me. He said that the freezing level will affect the Sauk and Skagit more than rain. And that, if the freezing level isn't too high, one or the other will still be in shape. With that in mind, I headed to the Sauk, albeit with low expectations.

When I reached the river, I felt that I was out of luck. The water was visibly rising and opaque. At that point I determined to head for Rockport to see what the Skagit was doing. But my car decided to turn at the bridge crossing the Sauk south of Rockport and take the gravel road to what is known as the Native Hole. When I stood on the dirt slide that serves as a boat launch, I felt as though I was really out of luck. In fact, that gray water snuffed out any hopes I had left. I think my despair was complete enough to satisfy the river gods because, as I turned away from the river, a big fish rolled violently in the shallows directly in front of me.

I scrambled for my rod and desperately waded into the hole above my new-found spot. Hope had returned, but it wasn't a deep feeling of confidence, rather a mocking sort of feeling that I had nothing to lose.

When I stepped in the river, I stopped only long enough to tie on a huge hot-orange "native getter" that I'd tied under a Coleman lantern at Mike Kinney's cabin. Since the river had me backed up against the alders, casting was terrible—I flipped and flapped my sink-tip around the trees in my way until I got the fly and tip out into the flow. These efforts were nearly, but not quite, futile. So the old despair returned again. That's probably why I got bit...the despair. Actually, it wasn't even a strike, more like a snag.

It's astonishing to have a heavy snag start to buck and splash, especially when you are in the depths of despair. Right away I saw a thick green back and a big snout churning and squirming twenty feet away. My first impression was that, oh jeez, it's some lost king salmon or freak chum. It was too big to be a steely. In the first few seconds, I somehow convinced myself that this was some kind of big weird salmon that runs in the spring. Funny how our senses are overpowered by our reason—or lack of reason.

The fish never ran more than thirty feet, it never jumped clear, and it never held still. Doing battle with the chum salmon of November was still clear in my mind, and I used that experience to fight this fish and, eventually, to drag it close enough for a grab. I turned the fish in to shore at the absolute limit of my leader. An attempt to use the backbone of the rod would have broken it. I just pointed my tip at the fish and ground away at the reel, dead convinced that this wasn't a steelhead.

The coral gill plates and square tail (I can still see them) should have convinced me. But, if they had, I probably would've eased off and never gotten hold of my monster. As it went, I forced him in close, saw his foot-long snout and made a grab. I wound up sitting in the river with a grip on the fish's lower jaw (bad move, unless you like infected cuts across your palm and fingers) and the wrist of his tail.

I have long fingers, but I could barely span one side of his tail. I leaned (or fell) back and hugged him to me. This is when I realized it really was a steelhead. By far the biggest I'd ever seen. Bigger than ANY king or chum salmon I'd caught. There's a strange sad feeling you get at a time like this. You feel like an intruder who is being tolerated for only a minute. You feel like you don't belong here, you don't deserve this, and you should go home and shut up because you're puny and insignificant.

I freed my tenuous tail-hold, pulled the rod out of the water, and held it against his flank. His nose came to a point well passed the first guide on my two-handed rod. I pinched my rod at that point and let go of my jaw hold. The fish slid off me (I was nearly lying down in the water at this point) and into the river where he broke away with a whoosh. That's where I sat for a very long time.

I closed my eyes and all I could see was pink cheeks, a huge flank, and a square tail the size of a dustpan. A big dustpan. I was still sitting in the water when a car door slammed behind me. I turned to look. A guy was already standing there. The customary greeting was on his lips when I yelled (far too loudly), "YOU GOTTA TAPE MEASURE?" The sentence must have sounded like one long word.

Being one of the more experienced old hands on the river, he knew from my bugging eyes and trembling lips what had happened. Without a word he returned to his car, rummaged around, and came back to me. When he walked down the slide, I realized that my fingers hurt from pinching the rod at the mark. I then did something I've never done before, or since. I slid my pinch a few inches toward the butt of the rod. I really doubted my eyes at this point and I truly expected derision or disbelief. So I fudged a little in the name of credibility.

The man held the tape up to my fish mark and said, "Thirty-nine inches, maybe forty if you move your thumb—whatta fish!" That's when another fish rolled so close I nearly felt it. I just stared—at the man, at my white fingers still pinching the rod, at the water. My new friend read my face like a book and said, with a shrug, "When you're hot, you're hot. Get 'em." He turned to his car.

My tippet was chewed up and I wanted to save the fly, so I cut off the tippet to change out. I couldn't tie a blood knot (trembling hands), so I gave up and tied another "big native getter" right to the twelve-pound section of my leader. The pads in my new disk-drag reel were greasy and wet. This caused it to backlash when I set the hook on my next fish. Same spot, same flow, another monster. I had loops and coils hanging out of my reel when the fight began.

This fish stayed put long enough for all three of us to gape at my loopy, messed-up reel. The fish, me, and the old man all froze for the classic moment suspended in time. Then the fish exploded away from me with his back bulging the water and his tail churning like a big boat propeller. The loops and tangles locked up and bound the reel against the fish's surge. He pulled me into the river until the current took my footing and I could go no further. He porposed against my line like a vicious dog on a short chain until the leader broke.

In five seconds that fish completely destroyed a spool of flyline. The loops and hitches were sunk so deeply that I had to cut the whole works out with a knife.

When the leader let go, I turned to see if my new acquaintance was still watching. He was. I'll always admire the way he said, "I knew you'd hook 'nother," and left.

The Skagit and its Fishery: Environmental Issues

Robert T. McLaughlin, a Washington resident since birth, is a casual acquaintance of mine whom I have respected for many years. He is an active member of the Steelhead Committee of The Federation of Fly Fishers, a group of politically active fly fishermen whose slogan is "Dedicated to the Preservation of Wild Steelhead." Bob has been an avid fly fisherman for over 30 years, but, in recent years, has been spending more time working "for" the fish than fishing. That is the reason I asked him to share with us, in his words, some of the environmental and conservational issues concerning the Skagit River watershed. Bob's writing, like the articles he has written for numerous publications, tells the story like it is.

Robert McLaughlin

Angler and author Roderick Haig-Brown once stated, "Perhaps fishing is just a reason to be near rivers." For many anglers, fishing is a reason to be near the Skagit. Success may be greater on other area streams, yet anglers return each season.

* * *

Massive clear-cutting has grossly contributed to the loss of spawning habitat within the watershed.

I have enjoyed the fall sunshine and autumn colors of the lazy, broad, farm bordered, lower river. I have been spellbound in the surrealism of a foggy morning while drifting silently in the estuary. But the upper river is best for my soul, where hills and mountains draw close and civilization is less present. There is no better time on this beautiful river than the March/April catch-and-release steelhead season.

Yet because of human carelessness I grieve for what might have been. Total preservation isn't what I long for. I want a compromise, some sense of a land ethic, which would farm our fish and forests instead of mining them. Now, I believe, we are just beginning to turn our resource policies towards a more sane and balanced course.

Morning sun casts its light on the head end of Dutchmen flat, Skagit River.

The river's aesthetic value, as well as its fish and timber resources, have been assaulted by poorly designed dams and rapacious logging practices. Three Seattle City Light power dams block and interrupt proper flows high on the river. At Concrete, two Puget Power dams block the Baker River, a sizeable tributary of the Skagit. I spoke with an employee at the mouth of the Baker who had backed a small tank truck to the Skagit. He had trucked smolts, mostly salmon but a few steelhead, by the dams just as their parents were trucked up to the upper lake to seek spawning grounds in the tributaries. He told me how the upper dam was constructed with a collector ramp which gathered and spilled smolts over the dam. Years ago employees were proud that they got smolts over the dam, but countless thousands perished. With special efforts, Puget Power is seeing an increase of sockeye these days but without good fishways in the dams the resource is largely lost. I see ospreys make repeated forays into the smolt-laden waters. This increased predation is the result of an "artifishery."

An angler fishes the Sauk River during the Catch-and-Release season.

I squatted alongside a state fish biologist drawing maps in the sand on land of which I am part-owner. Yes, he says, we can dredge out a little creek, not because dredging is a biologist's favorite activity, but because logging upstream has so filled it with sediment that anadromous fish will no longer be able to ascend and spawn. The sand-filled stream flows into the powerful Sauk a short ways above the Skagit. Years of drought have caused glacial melting which in turn has put much more flour in the Sauk/Skagit than usual, but the logging degradation of spawning streams is far more damaging.

Finney Creek, a once wonderful stream, was devastated by logging, making one man say, "It made me want to cry." Jordan Creek, tributary to the Cascade which joins the Skagit at Marblemount was also blown out by improper logging.

Logging and other roads take their toll on the river also. Just look at the switchback visible from Highway 20 at Jackman Creek and you'll see the erosion streaming down the hill. It's destined for Jackman Creek and then for the Skagit. A few hundred yards away is where decades ago pioneer steelhead fly fisher Al Knudson hooked nine winter steelhead. He pointed his rod tip at the water and tried to muffle the sound of his reel to hide the activity from a fisherman below. Now stand at the culvert just above the Bennetville Bridge on the Darrington-Rockport Road and ask yourself how any fish could ascend the stream and reproduce.

Far downstream on tidal flats agriculture and dairying have carried the day, calling for diking to keep out the Skagit. The problem with this is that the dikes eliminate important nursery areas for juvenile salmonids. And, ironically, dikes keep the river in, when floods breach them and then aren't allowed to recede.

Much of the logging which has devastated the Skagit basin's fish runs has been done with the blessing of governmental entities—Washington State's Department of Natural Resources and the U.S. Forest Service. These lands belong to us. About one-third of anadromous fish descending the Skagit have been born in small tributaries which are so vulnerable to natural and human-made disasters.

Another environmental issue currently dividing people is the controversial Grandy Creek Hatchery. Ironically, this scheduled winter-run steelhead hatchery was budgeted by the legislature without a request from the Department of Fish and Wildlife. Generally, the department is lukewarm about this facility.

The department backed off when a coalition of fishing and environmental groups threatened to sue. They were not able to say with certainty that hatchery fish would not interact harmfully with wild stocks. But, at this writing, the money has been re-appropriated and the hatchery appears to be going forward. Sports anglers who want the facility are still hurting from the impact of the infamous Boldt Decision of 1974 in which certain treaty Indian tribes were guaranteed over one-half of salmon and steelhead; i.e one-half of a "paper run" projected by biologists.

There are indeed instances where hatchery fish have negatively impacted wild fish in various ways. Yet, two department steelhead biologists have told me that a January run of hatchery fish at Grandy Creek on the Skagit may well be a benign operation, about as safe as one can get. Meantime, hatchery steelhead production has been increasing at Marblemount with rearing at Barnaby Slough above Rockport, though because of netting and current low return ratios, the sport harvest is a shadow of former days. If Grandy Creek is built and works, it should provide more fish for sport fishers who wish to harvest them and might make the difference as to whether or not Indians will net wild fish.

One effort at enhancement of Skagit steelhead, now written off, was the catching of Skagit fish for broodstock, the progeny outplanted in tributaries as fingerlings. Pushed by locals to do so, the then area biologist was doubtful from the beginning, and proved himself correct. Biologists are convinced that the best plan is nature's plan: leave the wild fish alone to spawn as they will.

Yet fight for better habitat, culture ocean-going salmonids and restrict harvest as we may, recent years' escapements of fish have been scary. Something beyond our control and understanding, namely low ocean survival, seems to be nemesis of the wonderful fish of this wonderful river.

Still, I see hopeful signs, signs which stir some positive feelings within me, as do the chartreuse buds along the Skagit early in the spring.

It appears now that habitat may begin to be better cared for and wild fish valued more. Washington state has adopted a wild salmonid policy which, at least on paper, avows a greater concern for wild fish. The state has also combined two former agencies which separated management of salmon and steelhead and were not known for talking to each other. The state has revised its forest practice code with at least some improvements for streams and fish. The current Commissioner of Public Lands is a much more environmentally conscious person. Within the state government there is a watershed management plan wherein all related departments are beginning to work together where before stream and fisheries concerns were ignored in state policy. Biologists see some attitudinal change in the U.S. Forest Service. Offending culverts are being better engineered when county and state road work calls for replacement.

The above management issues dovetail with a comment by Curt Kraemer, the skilled and dedicated state biologist currently in charge of Skagit steelhead. I asked Curt, "Aside from a fix of

A bright male steelhead.

ocean conditions, if you had a magic wand, what would you have happen for the Skagit and its fish?"

Without hesitation he declared, "Better land stewardship throughout the basin."

If land stewardship (habitat) is important then so is another "h" and that is harvest. Some of us fishers have felt joy at the return in numbers of Dolly Varden in the Skagit system. They break up an otherwise slow day of steelheading with their take and tugging and finally the display of their silver and spots. They were declining badly, but a harvest regulation of no more than two fish a day over twenty inches allowed more fish to spawn and turned this tide.

Something that gives us hope that more fish will run to and spawn in the upper river is the fact that Seattle City Light has, in order to obtain a renewal of its dam licensing, agreed to allow more water and even flows in the upper river where there are no major tributaries to buffer the lack of water. Biologists believe that this will leave fewer fingerlings stranded by severe fluctuations.

How we fishers would love to have better angling in the beauty of the stream above Rockport and celebrate the presence of wild steelhead there. In *A River Runs Through It* Pastor Maclean kneels by the river with his sons. He tells them that the stones are eons old but that underneath the stones and older are the words of God. If they will get close and listen, he says, they will hear the words. If you listen to the Skagit, perhaps you will hear, and care. And if you care, perhaps you, along with many others, will become a keeper of the stream.

A Breakdown of River Sections

The following breakdown of river sections, including a discussion of the Sauk River, is intended to give a brief overview of the various floats one can make and to offer a better understanding of what to expect on each.

It's not my intent to hide any information regarding foot access to the many runs. But it would take a lot of space to detail roadside pullouts and trails. The pullouts and trails are not as obvious as they are on some other rivers.

Detailed descriptions of various runs and pools would be a waste of time. By the time you read this the water would have changed. This river system has a huge floodplain and is constantly undergoing change. Although specific pools may look the same after a period of high water or flood, holding lies within a pool may have been drastically altered. This change is part of the joy of these rivers.

The most experienced Skagit anglers have to relearn their river every season. If you are new to the Skagit and Sauk, adopt a pioneering spirit and explore like the rest of us do. If your time is limited...hire a guide.

Bacon Creek to Rockport

The Skagit River from Bacon Creek to the confluence of the Sauk is one of the most beautiful stretches of river anywhere on the planet. Without the glacial turbidity of the Sauk River and with three dams upstream to regulate the flow and filter out sediment, the river runs as clear as freshly polished glass. Water that is seemingly only a couple feet deep may be two to three times the assumed depth. The river bottom is fairly infertile, displaying its well-scoured rocky cobble as a virtual kaleidoscope of colors.

The river here is a joy to fish. One beautiful piece of fly water after the next. Whatever water type you enjoy fishing the most—barring boulder-strewn pocket water—you will find here in abundance.

The challenges that lie in this thirteen-mile stretch of water begin with its clarity. It's often heard among fly angling circles that the river above the Sauk doesn't hold many fish. Yet gear fishermen (primarily plug pullers) do quite well here at times. So, it's not so much a lack of fish as it is a lack of finding fish in water suited to fly fishing. That's not to say that fish can't be taken on flies here; they certainly can and are. It's just a bit more unforgiving than fishing below the Sauk. Simply put, the clear water forces the majority of fish to hold in deep or heavy flows that may or may not be within reach of a fly.

Concentrate your efforts in low-light situations like mornings, evenings, overcast days, or shaded areas. Don't overlook tumultuous water as protective cover, particularly on sunny days. Sounds like steelheading in general doesn't it? It is. Yet many people are intimidated by the gin-clear water on this stretch. Which is a good thing for those of us who enjoy fishing where there is plenty of water and few fishermen.

Fishing in February snowstorm, Sauk River.

Access to the many runs is relatively easy. Highway 20 runs right along the north bank of the river and Martin Road along the south. Floating in a raft or drift boat is a great way to spend the day and cover a lot of water. There is a boat launch on the south side of the river in Marblemount. It lies directly under the steel bridge that crosses the Skagit. From here it's an eight-mile float to the ramp at Howard Miller Steelhead Park in Rockport. Although an easy float that is suitable for novice boaters, care should be taken as the river is deceptively fast and contains several log jams that can sneak up on you in a hurry. Stay alert.

Rockport to Concrete

To many who fish the Skagit, the nine miles from Rockport downstream to Concrete are synonymous with its name. For here lie noted runs like The Mixer, Larson's, Sauk Store, Dutchmen, and Jackman Creek. All are downriver from the Sauk, all are classic fly drifts.

In addition to these famous runs, there are many other places to drift a fly in this stretch. Some obvious, others very subtle. The key is to fish anything that even remotely looks like it might have the potential to hold a resting fish, no matter how big or small. Simply assessing a piece of water from shore won't tell you a thing—you have to go down and fish it. It's big water, and hold-ing lies are not as clearly defined as in smaller streams.

To the uninitiated getting to the water on this stretch may be difficult. Highway 20 runs along the north bank, and South Skagit Highway parallels the south, yet roadside pullouts are not very obvious and thick riparian growth often obstructs your view of the river. The best advice I can give is to float the river in a drift boat or raft. It's easy water that even the most inexperienced boater can handle.

For a full-day float, launch at Howard Miller Steelhead Park and take out at the launch in Concrete where the Baker River joins the Skagit. A nice half-day float would be to launch at the park and float four miles to Faber's Landing.

The Lower River

Because the Skagit is closed to fishing below the Dalles Bridge in Concrete during the catch-and-release season, anglers often refer to anything downstream of the bridge as the lower river. In actuality there are still roughly 40 miles of river below Concrete before it empties into the bay. Although the pools are few and far between, good fly water can be found in twenty of these miles. The water downriver of Sedro-Woolley is better left to the plunkers.

Mount Baker and Skagit River. Mount Baker, an active volcano, is the tallest peak within the watershed at 10,773 feet.

people prefer to fish the well-defined runs and holding lies of the Sauk over the Skagit. Although it is a formidable river, the Sauk is much smaller than the Skagit so it is not as intimidating to fish. You get the feeling that you have a little more control over your fly's destiny. Of course, that doesn't mean that the Sauk gives up its fish easily.

I fished the Sauk for two winters and springs before I landed my first fish. It seems that whenever fish were in the river, I found it to be out of shape or marginally fishable. When fish were scarce, of course, the river was running clear and beautiful. This is often the case with the Sauk.

The river is glacially fed and unpredictable. Even the smallest amount of rain can turn the river into a pewter-colored torrent. Glacial runoff is natural to the Sauk, but massive clearcuts are not. Reckless logging practices

Once again, the river is paralleled by highways on both sides of the river. The only reasonable floats one should consider making would be Concrete to Birdsview, or Birdsview to Hamilton. Just remember that winter days are short, the runs long, and it's a slow float between them.

Remember to check state fishing regulations. This stretch of river traditionally closes on March 15 but may be closed earlier in the future.

The Sauk River

Originating in the Glacier Peak Wilderness, the Sauk River is free of dams and should continue to flow unhindered due to its designation under the National Wild and Scenic Rivers Act of 1968.

The Sauk is truly a gem of a river. Wild and unruly its character is far different from that of the Skagit. It is a steelheader's paradise nonetheless. In fact, many

Lunch-time rendezvous. Sauk Mountain towers in the background.

have denuded the hillsides which further contributes to the unstable flows.

March and April are the best months to fish the Sauk for wild steelhead. They are also good months for rain. Some seasons find the Sauk fishable for only a couple of days. Fortunately the Sauk clears quickly after the rain subsides. The optimum time to be fishing the Sauk is as it's dropping and clearing.

The Sauk and its many tributaries provide the spawning grounds for over half of the Skagit's remaining wild winter steelhead. If you can find the Sauk in shape, it's probably not a bad idea to fish it and fish it hard. The window of opportunity is rarely a big one.

The catch-and-release season begins March 1 and, just like the Skagit, closes April 30. Fishing is not allowed above the Darrington Bridge during this special season. Highway 530 runs along the Sauk, providing foot access to various stretches of river. There are three floats you can make.

A black-tailed deer crosses the river while an angler watches.

But, first, a word of caution. The Sauk is NOT for the inexperienced boater. Large exposed boulders, log jams, sweepers, braided channels and swift tumultuous flows make the Sauk a very technical and dangerous river. I speak from experience. During the 1995 season, after countless hours of running the Sauk without incident, I got complacent and came very close to capsizing my boat. We came out just fine in the end, but I was pretty shaken. It was, however, a good reminder to me of just how fast the Sauk can eat you up.

With sound boating skills and a huge amount of respect, a day spent floating and fishing the Sauk River is as great an experience as any steelheader could hope for.

There are three public boat launches on the Sauk. All are primitive and require a little sweat and ingenuity to successfully

The Skagit downstream of Gorge Powerhouse.

put in and take out a drift boat. The first is located at the Darrington Bridge next to the mill. The next is at the confluence of the Suiattle River. The third and last is on the west side of the river just upstream from where the South Skagit Highway crosses the Sauk. By putting in at this launch, you can fish both the Sauk and the Skagit on a single float. The takeout is at Faber's landing on the south side of the Skagit River.

Any one of the three floats is just the right length for a full day's fishing. One is not necessarily better than the next. They all have unique personalities, and fish can be anywhere in them.

Food, Accommodations, and Fly Shops

The Skagit is by no means off the beaten path. Accommodations are plentiful. There is a choice of motels and restaurants in Concrete, Rockport and Marblemount. In Concrete I recommend the North Cascade Inn Restaurant and Lounge (360) 853-8870. Rockport is limited to one motel—The River House (360) 853-8557. It has a restaurant that's only open on the weekends. The best place to stay in Marblemount is Clark's Skagit River Resort (360) 873-2250, otherwise known as the "bunny farm." Huge domestic rabbits live freely on the grounds surrounding the rental cabins. The rabbits are quite tame and always looking for a handout.

Don't expect to find gourmet food in any of these places. Backwoods Americana is always on the menu. You could, of course, cook for yourself. Clark's has rooms with kitchens, and you can camp at Howard Miller Steelhead Park.

Howard Miller was a Skagit County commissioner from the late 1960s into the '70s. And, much to the delight of Skagit recreational users, he was a prominent steelhead guide on the Skagit for more than 25 years. Now living the retired life in Sedro-Woolley, Howard can look back at his many accomplishments both on the water and off. His greatest gift to us was fulfilling the need for a "place where fishermen and boaters had a good place to launch their boats, and then have a nice place to get a shower and camp at the end of the day." That's exactly what Howard Miller Steelhead Park in Rockport is.

The park is affectionately called "Club Rockport" by some local anglers. Steelhead fishers flock to the park in spring, staying in R.V.s, trailers, or tents. Friendly gatherings are a nightly occurrence and I'll be darned if an occasional party doesn't break out. Of course, these are sedate parties—we wouldn't want to oversleep! If you plan on staying at the park, it would be wise to reserve a site well ahead of time. Write or call Howard Miller Steelhead Park, Box 127, Rockport, WA 98283 (360) 853-8808.

Some of the local stores carry limited gear-fishing tackle, but don't expect to find anything in the fly department. The nearest fly shop is in Mount Vernon. If you plan on visiting the Skagit no trip would be complete without a stop at Skagit Anglers, 315-G Main Street, Mount Vernon, WA 98273 (360) 336-3232. Skagit Anglers is the only fly shop in Skagit county and a good one at that. A complete line of name-brand equipment, along with friendly up-to-date fishing information, is available Monday through Saturday from 9:00 a.m. to 5:30 p.m., Thursday and Friday the doors stay open until 7:00 p.m.

Guides

A call to any of the Seattle-area fly shops can put you in touch with someone to guide you on the various Puget Sound rivers.

There are only three men who guide the Sauk and Skagit full time. A day spent on the river with any of them is a unique and enriching experience. All are superb instructors and keen interpreters of river lore.

John Farrar is a well-known figure. A flamboyant character who, to me, epitomizes the sport of steelhead fly fishing. John and his partner, Bob Aid, started guiding the Skagit about the same time the catch-and-release season started in the early '80s (Bob now works for Kaufmann's Streamborn in Seattle and still does some guiding). John Farrar can be reached at (206) 367-2243.

Mike Kinney lives on the banks of the Stillaguamish River and is highly respected as one of the Northwest's best steelheaders. I've known Mike for close to ten years and every time I see him, I learn something new. He can be reached at (206) 435-3778.

I am last of the trio. My number is (360) 428-8726. Like John and Mike, I place a strong emphasis on instruction and complete appreciation of all natural aspects of the river. The three of us are proponents of the two handed rod and adept at teaching its use.

For a great steelheading experience, give any one of us a call well in advance of the season.

<hr />

Skagit Anglers: The only fly shop in Skagit County is located in Mount Vernon.